Mastering Your Inner Game

BOB DONNELL

DEDICATION

This book is dedicated to my children: Brittney, Justin, Austin & Macy You all have been and are my constant in life and I love you and am thankful for the honor of being your dad!

CONTENTS

INTRODUCTION

Welcome to Mastering Your Inner Game. I'm Bob Donnell of Next Level Live. It's my privilege and honor to work with you for the next seven days and really help you identify what your Inner Game is, where it's at now, and where you need it to be so you can get the results that you truly want in every area of your life.

This isn't just about business, but this isn't just about money, it's not just about relationships, it's not about spiritual commission, it's about whatever it is in your personal life that you want to create and make better. There's one thing I know, that no matter what level you're at, there's always a Next Level. No matter how much money you have, no matter how great your relationship, there's always one area (or more) of your life that you want to get better in! That's what this program is for. It's called Mastering Your Inner Game!

So let's get started, day one is all about commitment. Let me ask you this, why did you pick up this book? Look, there are a million programs out there, why did you join this one? There are programs that are audio. There are programs that are video. There are programs that are in-person. There are programs that are recorded. There are programs that are books, and there are programs similar to this one. What is it that made you pick this one? Now, what is it that made you pick any program? I really want you to get in touch with what it is that you are trying to improve. What area of your life are you trying to improve? Is it your physical fitness, your health and vitality? Is it your spiritual connection, your relationship with other people? Is it your business, your finances? What is it? I really want you to be clear on what is that you're trying to improve and really work on and get the results.

Now, let me tell you, this is not going to be easy. I don't want you to think that this is going to be easy. It's not, and it's going to be uncomfortable. Look, the first time you went to the gym you were probably a little bit sore. You were probably sore for several times going to gym, but at one point you got to the point where you weren't sore from going to the gym anymore, so you decided to push yourself to the next level and became sore again. So what's this all about? Any time you start to really step out, you're going to create that uncomfortable feeling for a period of time. What I can guarantee to you is that once we move past that comfort level and start to get uncomfortable, that we'll start achieving greater results, greater results in every aspect that you're wanting to succeed on, so let's get started.

SESSION ONE: COMMITMENT

Commitment, it's not easy, it's not going to be comfortable, but it's going to give you the results that you want. That's why the first thing I asked you is what it is that you're trying to improve, and what it is that you're trying to get better at. If you've got that reminder, if you've got that anchor to go back to, then when things get tough, things get a bit uncomfortable, you'll be able to get recommitted.

Let's talk about commitment. Let me ask you to think about three things in commitment. First, let me ask you to think about a person, a person that exemplifies the word commitment to you. Maybe it's someone you know; maybe it's someone you don't know. Maybe it's someone you saw on *Time Magazine*; maybe it was someone like Mother Theresa. Whoever it is that you've identified really reeks of the word commitment, that's the word, that's the person that would be next to that word in the dictionary. Who is that person? Be very clear on that person. Think about that person. Can you see their face; can you see who they are? Once you've done that find a picture of them, maybe from the magazine, an old picture of someone you know.

Look, this is really serious. If you want the greatest results you're going to have to dig deep, take some time to do exercises. I will never give you exercises that are going to take you more than like 15–20 minutes a day, but I can guarantee that if you spend the 15-20 minutes, invest in yourself in the 15-20 minutes, the results will be amazing. I guarantee it.

So here's what I want you to do, think about the person. Now I want you to think about this, think about a word other than the word commitment that really makes you think committed, commitment. Maybe it's just another word, but what I want you to do is think about another word that exemplifies the word commitment to you. It could be someone's name, it could be a thought, whatever it is, think about that one thing, that one word, which really exemplifies commitment to you. Write that down, put it on a piece of paper, and make sure that you have that with you so it's a constant reminder.

So you have the picture, you have the word, now here's the last thing I want you to do. I want you to think of a picture that's not a portrait, maybe it's a golfer, maybe it's somebody stretching for the finish line, whatever it is, I want you to think of a picture that exemplifies commitment to you. What is that picture? Think of it, go online, download, and print that picture. Put that picture next to your computer, in your day timer, whatever it is that's going to be a constant reminder to you.

Now, you have a person, you have a picture, and you have a word. Those three things are going to be your anchors. Those are going to be those things that on those days when you don't feel like getting up and going to the gym, when you don't feel like getting up and being nice to someone, when you don't feel like getting up and going to work and making those extra sales calls, those are going to be the anchors to remind you what is commitment. Am I exemplifying that kind of commitment?

The next thing I want you to do, I want you to really think about when you talk to people whether it's your clients, your colleagues, your spouse, what kind of a level of commitment do you want from them, and what kind of a level of commitment do you expect from them? I'm serious, be serious about this.

Look, this isn't for me, this isn't for your family, this is for you. The best thing you can do here is be brutally honest with yourself. Become so transparent to yourself that you go that's me, or you really need to step up your game. If you're feeling like that, we're going to give you the tools and help to do that in the next seven days. So think about this, the term commitment. What kind of commitment do you expect from others, what kind of commitment do you expect from creditors, what kind of commitment do you expect from others you extend credit to? What kind of commitment do you expect from others? What kind of commitment do you expect from your spouse, your kids, your boss, and your employees? Is your commitment level higher, the same as, or less than that commitment that you're asking from someone else?

The reason it's important to be brutally honest with yourself here is because here's what happens. Sometimes we've convinced ourselves that we're getting a level of commitment that we're really not. What happens is when we go to expect a certain level of commitment from someone else our inner game begins to work and starts to unravel, because it begins to ask us how can you expect that from someone when you're not doing it yourself? How can you expect your kids to tell the truth when you're not telling the truth?

Be honest with yourself, be brutally honest with yourself. The thing that you've got to realize right now is that we've got to start being honest with ourselves to the point that we start to say it hurts, no more, I'm not going to deal with that. Not only that, but it's an underlying current. When we're not being honest with ourselves, it's that underlying current that's going on. Even when we're saying it to someone else, it's got this underlying current that's causing a disconnect between what you're saying and what you're doing, and it happens every day. If that happens, and you don't even realize it, now would be a great time to start realizing it. The next time you ask for someone's commitment on something, when you say "Okay do I have your word on it?" ask, hmm, when was the last time I broke my word?

Maybe you're asking for someone to say okay can you do this? And then say when was the last time I was asked to do this and I didn't do it? Maybe it's something on lying with your kids. Whatever it is, when you ask that of someone else, say, do I live up to that, or even a higher level? Or, do I ask something that I'm not willing to give myself?

Okay, now you've got the picture, you've got the word, and you've got the person, you've understood that the commitment, this underlying current, making sure that you're expecting the same or less than what you're giving, you've got to be that committed.

Now let me ask you this, have you ever known someone that talks a really good game? They say they're committed but they're not? They say I'm working, I'm working, but you look at them and you go you're not working. You're hanging out at the computer, you're hanging out at the coffee pot, and you're not really working. Look, don't let yourself fall victim to that. You've got to be brutally honest with yourself; you've got to understand it.

Now, we've all heard the joke. Who's more committed to the breakfast you eat? The chicken that lays the egg or the pig that gives his life for the bacon or sausage? Folks, we know the answer to that. Who's more committed? Now, what kind of level are you giving to yourself, to your finances, to your relationships with other people? Are you just being a chicken, or are you putting everything in?

If you've ever watched poker, you've seen all in. They push everything to the front of the table, all their money, everything is in. Are you that committed? And if you're not, you've got to get that committed. Let me ask you this, if you don't do this program, if this doesn't work for you, what's it going to cost you? I've had people say, "Bob, I'm thinking about getting a part time job, I'm a realtor and things are tough." Do you know what I tell them? Go get a full time job, because once you started thinking that way, there's a greater chance that you're going to just go and get a job anyways, and you're probably going to end up leaving real estate. Do the real estate community a favor. Now look, there are times where you just have to take a part time job to do things, I'm not talking about that. I understand there are times where you may be ambitious to do more; I'm not talking about that. 9 times out of 10 when you let your brain go to if it doesn't work, oh well, it's not going to work.

So look, this program, it's going to cost you if you don't make this work for you. If you don't take the full on commitment to make this work, what's it going to cost you? Because you've got to be clear on that. If you're clear on how much it's going to cost you. If it's going to cost you your right arm, you'll probably do it. If it's going to cost you a tennis shoe that you can go replace, it's probably not going to cost you a lot. You've got to be really clear, what's it going to cost you if you don't take the necessary actions to make this work? You've got to become committed; you've got to become committed on every level.

You know I had a coaching client that used to play in the NFL, used to play football. He had gone into Real Estate and mortgages after retiring from football, pro-bowl player, and great guy. He just wasn't doing well. He said, "Bob, I'm not doing so well, I don't know what's going on." We had a couple of sessions and I asked him, on a scale of 1 to 10, what level of effort do you put in your real estate and mortgage business on a daily basis? What level of effort? He said, "Bob, honestly a level 4." A level 4, how far would you have made it in football at a level 4? And he said, "I would have never made it out of Pop Warner." Ding, a light went on. He went "oh my gosh."

Folks, what I find time and time again are that people are expecting NFL results and giving Pop Warner effort. Make sure that the amount of effort you're willing to give is strong enough to get the results you desire. If it's not, you're going to have to choose one of two things. I can't be anymore simple than this. You've got to just get this picture. You're going to have to be willing to settle for less, or increase your productivity, increase your effort, your drive, your determination, and the amount of commitment you're willing to give. Increase your commitment, or decrease what you're trying to get. It's plain and simple. The easiest way I can explain it.

So let me ask you this, what is it going to take for you to become fully committed to your business? When you're all in, and totally bought into this system. What is it going to take for you to become fully committed to your business, your life, your relationship? Whatever it is that you said in the beginning you wanted to increase, what is it going to take to get to that level where you're totally committed, you're on fire, you're set, I'm going to do this no matter what? What if I told you that if you didn't do this that one of your most loved people in your life was going to die if you didn't take every action that was necessary to get the result you want? If that was going to be the cost, would you do it? My guess is yes, because that was more important. Saving that person's life was more important than not doing it, taking the shortcut, sleeping in a little bit later, not going to the gym. That person's life was more important than the uncomfortable of having to do the things necessary to get the results you wanted. We can't create that type of urgency on everything that we do in our lives, but we can certainly simulate it. We can certainly get it to the point where we begin to take more actions to get the results that we want.

So think about it, what are the things that it's going to cost you if you don't do what we're talking about today? If you don't get that committed, what's it going to cost you? Now, there's another thing to look at and that's the benefit. What's the benefit if I do this?

The only reason I start with the cost is because studies have shown that between six and seven times the cost of not doing something, the pain of regret, is a far greater motivator than the pursuit of happiness. If that's the case, let's think about what's it going to cost you if it doesn't happen. If you say I want to grow my business, let me ask you this, what's it going to cost if you don't? Well you know, I'm not going to be able to make that trip to Europe next year. It's probably not going to happen. But, if you say you know, my daughter's graduating from high school this year and she's going to want to go to college, and I need to step up my game to be able to provide for my daughter to go to college, there's a good chance that you will. If you're thinking along those lines, let me ask you this, imagine, the day that your daughter gets accepted to Yale, Harvard, whatever school it is. Maybe it's your college, your Alma Mater, she's always wanted to go to your Alma Mater and you say yes, I want to help her get to my Alma Mater. She says daddy, I got accepted, look I got accepted, I worked so hard for four years. What's it going to feel like if you have to look at her in the face and say you know, I wish I could send you there but I just don't have the money? I could have stepped up my game, I could have worked harder, I could have gotten the results that would allow you to go but honey, I just didn't. I'm sorry. What's it going to feel like? What emotion is that going to bring up inside you? Are you in touch with that? You've got to connect with that kind of emotion where you say that's it; I'm not going to allow that to happen. I'm not willing to face my daughter and tell her no I can't send you to school. I know you worked for 4 years but daddy didn't work hard enough, daddy didn't step up his game.

Folks, we've got to get real, and we've got to get to that point where we begin to connect the dots so that we start getting the results that we want. The first level of this is commitment. You've got to be committed.

Now let me ask you this, if you do fully go all in, what's it going to be like? What's your life going to be like? What are your relationships with people going to be like? What's your business going to be like? What's your spiritual connection going to be like? I mean really think about that, what's it going to do for your life, what's it going to do for your business, and what's it going to do for your business if you go all in? Do you have a picture of that? I want you to be really clear on that, because once have a very clear picture of that, it's just around the corner.

Now, the next six days are going to be explosive days for you. Don't forget to do the exercises every day. First, cut out the pictures of the person, the word, the image of what commitment looks like. Second, write down what you would be willing to fight to the death for. What would you be willing to fight to the death for? For me, it's my belief system, my faith in God, my relationship with Jesus Christ. What would you be willing to die for? I would also be willing to die for my children, but there are very few things in my life I would be willing to die for. Probably, very few things you would be willing to die for as well. Those are called non-negotiable. I want you to be very clear right now on what is it that you would die for? What is it that would go in? Start associating, start putting in those anchors. We're going to work on this over the next 6 days. We're going to start really honing in on how you anchor back to these emotions, so we start getting the results we want. Do the exercises, be committed to yourself, be real, totally honest with yourself. Tomorrow morning you're going to get the next video. By that time, I want you to have done the work; I want you to have written down these things, cut out these pictures. Take 15-20 minutes, it's not going to take long. Aren't you worth it? Aren't the relationships you want to improve worth it? Isn't the business you want worth it? Of course it is. So take the time, make the commitment, go all in, and I'll see you tomorrow morning. Until then, enjoy your next level.

SESSION TWO: DESIRE

Welcome to day two. Day two of creating your winning inner game. You made it. You made it through day one. Now let me ask you, did you do the exercises? Did you really realize what it takes to make a commitment? Did you realize what areas of your life where you could have made a stronger commitment and you didn't? Did you start catching yourself throughout the day as to say am I expecting other people to be more committed than I am? Am I expecting more of other people than I'm willing to give to myself? If you did, you're on your way.

Now day two, day two is about desire. Desire. Now, when we hear the word desire we're always thinking about the desire of the person of the opposite sex or the desire for money. We almost look at is as greed. I'm going to talk to you about desire, the first time that maybe you were in love, or you have a desire to meet someone. I want to talk about what that felt like. Do you remember? Think back maybe when you were a teenager that you had a desire to spend every waking moment with that girl or guy of your dreams. Or, maybe you had such an intense desire to just be with them and talk. Think about when you would sit on the phone for hours and hours and talk to them. Think about that time, how much you desired to just hear that other person's voice. Or, think about something that keeps you up at night. Is there something that you intensely desire so much that you would be willing to stay up all night? I'm not talking about college where you pull an all-nighter to study. Those are things we just have to do; we're creating that sense of urgency because maybe we didn't study early. The bottom line is, I'm talking about that thing that keeps you up at night.

Think about when you were a kid and Christmas Eve, do you remember staying awake because you had such a desire for Christmas morning to come? Do you remember when you were turning 15 or 16 and you were thinking about getting your license and having a desire for it? I'm seeing a lot of people now that maybe they're not as excited about getting their license because of all the things that have gone on, but I remember when I was 15 or 16 and I couldn't wait to get my license, and I bet you were probably the same way. What was that desire like? What made you think and feel so emotional that you couldn't sleep? What made you feel so emotional that you just couldn't wait to get your license? Now, I want you to think, what in your life right now is like oxygen, that if it was taken away from you, you would fight; you would do anything you could to get it back. What is like that for you? More and more people are saying, well that's not my job, it's not my relationship, it's not this, and it's not that. What IS like that to you? I can guarantee that if I put a pillow over your face you would fight me to the death to try and get me away from you so that you could feel and breathe and live. What is it that if it was taken away from you, it would almost feel like someone cut off your oxygen.

For me, it's impacting people, speaking, and going out and imparting vision, and sharing with people some of the experiences I've had and how they made me into the person I am today. Maybe that's not it for you, but what is it? Maybe it's your ability to be with your kids. Maybe it's your ability to connect deeply with another person. This morning, one of my coaching clients and I were talking and she was talking about how amazing of a week she had. The reason she had an amazing week wasn't because she came into a bunch of money, the reason was because she really felt like she had an opportunity to connect deeply with several people this week, and that's what drives her, that's what stirs her to the core.

What is it for you? What is it for you that it's like oxygen, if it were to be taken away life would seem like it's not worth living? What is that? Is it your ability to share? Is it your ability to communicate? Is it your ability to love? Is it your relationship with God? What is it that is so strong that if it were taken away it would not be worth going on? I want you to think about those things that really stir you, those things that in the past have made you feel unstoppable. DO you remember a time where you felt unstoppable? Probably because you had an intense desire, something was coming between you and what you wanted, and whatever it was you were willing to break through that barrier to get there, probably because you had an intense desire, and that's what I'm talking about.

Do you remember when you were getting your first car, how excited you were? Now, isn't it funny that some of our first cars were really pieces of junk? But, we were excited about them because they represented something to us. What was it that the car represented? For many of us it represented freedom, the opportunity to get away from home. For many of us it represented an opportunity to date, to go out, and to see our friends. Whatever it was, for many of us it represented far more than just getting a car. That underlying current was creating a desire that was so strong within us that there were times I bet you did things you didn't want to do in order to put gas in that car or make that payment or buy that car.

Do you remember your first job, being excited about your job, and wanting it so bad that when you got it you were like yes! I'm in, I'm going to work. I remember so many young people who have said I can't wait to get out of high school because I'm going to work every day and I'm going to love it because I'm going to get paid for school. Only a few years later they're working every day and you call them up and they said oh man, all I do is work. The desire shifted. When they were first getting it they were excited about it.

Maybe you're in a career right now, a relationship right now, maybe even a business right now, and the newness has worn off. You don't feel that desire. Changing your inner game and creating a winning inner game is finding that desire again. I know a lot of people that have vision boards, a lot of great pictures of things they love, they have all these things, and over a period of time I find some of those things don't mean as much as they did before, so people begin to lose that desire. It's not that they don't want it anymore, but their desire has decreased, and it's no longer serving them the way that it once did. Maybe you've got a picture of a Mercedes and you're not as crazy about it. Take it down, whatever it is; put something on there that really means something to you. Every time you look at it ah yah it's that, you feel it. Whatever that is for you. It doesn't have to be a material thing, it might just be time spent with your kids, time spent with your parents. I want you to have a picture of that, cut it out, paint one, whatever you need to do to create an image that your mind can realize what that image is. Yesterday we talked about commitment, putting those images always before us so that we stay focused on those things. Creating this desire.

In the next 5 days we're going to talk about several other things that are going to help create your inner winning game. Your inner winning game has to start with your commitment and your desire. It doesn't have to be money, it doesn't have to be material possessions, but it's got to be something that you know deep down inside you ache for, you long for, you want.

Let me tell you a little secret, I know a lot of people who tell me "Bob, I don't know what I want anymore." If you're feeling that way, you're not alone. There are a lot of people that don't know what they want anymore. In order to find out what you want, you might have to think about what is it that you don't want. I know that I don't want to be separated from my kids. I know that I don't want to be alone for the rest of my life. I know that I don't want to be bankrupt. You might have to think about what you don't want in order for you to start to be able to paint a picture that shows what you do want. If that's you, that's okay. Start thinking about what you don't want. If that's what I don't want, obviously I want something else. That's going to help lead you in the direction of some of the things you want.

Now ultimately, Rick Warren wrote a masterful book, right? All about purpose. For most people what they really want is they want to feel important. Most people want to have a purpose. Last night one of my friends and I were talking, we talked about the fact of leaving a legacy. Some people just want to leave a legacy. Some people just want something that goes beyond their time on earth. Maybe that's you. Maybe it's a legacy that you're looking to leave. Maybe you're just trying to find a purpose. Maybe you just want to feel important. Whatever it is, those things are going to have to create a desire.

Imagine it was you just want to feel important. Now, the best way to create a desire is to say what would that feel like if I felt important. What would that look like? How would I walk? How would I speak? What words would people use to describe me if I felt important? Again, once you begin to put yourself into that model and feel the emotion of that, all of a sudden you create a desire. But, sometimes that desire has got to come from deep within, and sometimes it's got to be something we create by using mental imagining, by using pictures, by using words. By using associations where our brain is connecting with something else that spurs with our desire and brings it up to the surface. If that's you, it's okay, but you've got to do it. You've got to find that desire. You've got to create that deep within, and explore every ounce of it.

Do you notice I'm speaking so passionately today? Why? It's because desire is such a tricky subject for some people. I don't know what I want. If you don't, my guess is that you do. My guess is that you do know what you want. What you want is to feel important. What you want is to feel accepted. What you want is to feel loved. There are several things that I guarantee you as a human being know what you want. Start with that, start with that and create that desire that what would that feel like, what would that be like? What is it like for me to feel important, to feel loved, accepted, and appreciated?

Create the desire, build upon it. Here's what I want you to do, I want you to dream build. If you've decided that you want to feel loved, appreciated, and important. Or, maybe you've decided that you want to create an amazing income and leave millions to a charity, or spend more time with your loved ones. Whatever it is, I want you to help build that desire by creating what I call dream building by literally taking a look at others who are living that life and what they are like. Find somebody that's living that life, somebody who looks important, feels important, is making the kind of money you want, and living the kind of life you want.

Several years ago I decided that I wanted to create a business that I could do to anywhere, from anywhere, and I could create residual models. The most exciting thing for me is I wanted to be able to do it from anywhere. I didn't want to do it from an office; I didn't want to have to be in the same place every day. I wanted to be able to travel and do things, and this business has allowed me to do that. It came with a lot of thought and what I wanted was three things: a business that I could do to anywhere, from anywhere, and have a residual model. I now knew that I had to put together a recipe of a program that would allow me to do those things. I had to dream build, I had to take a look around and see what other people were doing that allowed them to do that kind of business. To create something from nothing.

Now, you're a lot more ahead than that, because I can guarantee whatever you're trying to do, wanting to do, whatever you're passionate about. Even if you don't know what you want to do, if you look at the things that you don't want to do or what you do want to do, the outcomes that you want to have, those 3 things are going to allow you to paint pictures or put pictures up that will stir you and move you, move you to a point of action even if you don't feel like taking action. Move you to getting up and going to the gym when you don't feel like going to the gym. Moving up and getting to the point where you say I've got to make 5 more sales calls today because you've got this dream. You've got this intense desire and sometimes you're just going to have to reach down, pull it up, and fulfill that desire. Because, when it feels like an oxygen mask that's being taken away, you'll fight with every ounce of energy you have in order to keep it.

So, enough about desire. I want you to explore every moment, every second of this day I want you to think about desire, what you truly desire above and beyond everything else. Write it down, put pictures up, and then we'll find a way to connect what you do with creating and getting what you want. But it starts with desire, go get it. Find that desire. Dig down deep. Today, make it a day all about desire. Looking through pictures, images, music. Exploring and finding other people that are living the life you want. Have that desire. Tomorrow, we'll talk about something else, but today is all about desire. Enjoy your next level.

SESSION THREE: SETTING YOURSELF UP TO WIN

Today we're going to talk about setting yourself up to win and doing the little things that you can do on a daily basis that will actually increase your opportunity to win. Now, as I was sharing in the monologue before, there are a lot of people that are really stressed. What's my passion, what's my purpose, what's my life mission, and all of these things, what I'm finding is more and more people don't know what they want, but they do know what they don't want. We're starting to look at things a bit differently with the transition in the economy in the past, with the market, with our business ventures, with the way things are happening in families. We're beginning to look at things a little differently and so we're going to talk about some of that today. We're going to talk about the things that are going to be necessary. This is my day 3 in my winning the inner game program, so you're going to actually see a preview of day 3 winning the inner game. It's not going to be exactly this, but it's going to be a lot of the same content.

Now let me ask you this, what do you do to set yourself up to win? What do you do on a daily basis to set yourself up to win? You might listen to some kind of music or you might make x amount of sales calls, you might read a little bit, you might study, you might get better in tune with what's going on in your market place. I really want to be specific about what you do to set yourself up to win. It's got to be consistent and persistent. If you're a member of Next Level you know my biggest focus is on consistent and persistent actions.

So let me ask you this, when was the last time you did something positive for someone and you felt pretty good about it? Did you feel good about it? Of course you did. The other day I was driving down the road and pulled into a parking lot and there was a car pulling out. I had the right away, but I stopped and let them go. I noticed I felt a little bit happier. I wasn't in any hurry, there wasn't a reason for me to rush through anyways, so what did it cost me to wait? It cost nothing. But it made me feel better about myself. I'm not saying that's going to revolutionize and change the way you think about yourself and erase all the garbage that has been placed on you from your childhood. What I'm talking about is starting to position yourself so that you can take these little actions on a daily basis.

Another thing is when my daughter died 12 years ago, I allowed myself to grieve, but I made myself get up and go do something positive for someone else. One thing I found was when I took my eyes off of me and put them on someone else I began to feel better about myself. As I began to feel better about myself, I started to do better and perform better in every area of my life.

So maybe you're struggling. Maybe you're struggling in sales, or losing weight, a relationship, maybe not just romantic, it could be with anyone. Any kind of relationship. Think about how you can set yourself up to win in those areas so as you are forced to stretch and become the person you were designed to be, you are able to do so more effectively because you have been positioning yourself to win.

Look, Wayne Gretskey, the greatest hockey player ever, has a great comment: good hockey players skate to where the puck is, but great hockey players skate to where the puck is going. What I like about that is it's not only applicable in hockey, but it's also applicable in business, relationships, finances, every area. Even in this area where we're talking about positioning ourselves and setting ourselves up to win, one of the things we need to do is be cognizant that the little things we do today are going to have an effect on us in the future.

You know, overspending one day or over a period of time can literally have huge ramifications. Saving a little bit at a time can have a huge ramification in the future. The things we're talking today are really doing those things that set us up to win.

Now let me ask you this. Can you tell me a song or a band or some kind of music that really stirs you to the core, really moves you? When you are in a funk you can listen to that and feel better, can you tell me what that is? If you can't, write that down. Think of the music that really moves you. Write it down, have it readily available to you. Have it on your CD player, MP3 player, whatever it is. Maybe it's a picture. I've got this great picture of this guy on the top of the mountain going YEAH! I love seeing that excitement and just knowing what he's accomplished by climbing to the mountain. That stirs me.

One of my coaching clients and a friend, he has an admiration for the way Tiger Woods plays golf. Tiger Woods, he has that fist pump and some great ways that he demonstrates and shows his emotions. We both like that aspect of Tiger. Maybe it's that picture. Maybe it's a movie. Maybe you've watched a movie and it really touched you. It moved me; it moved me to a state of emotion that I haven't felt in a while. I felt like I needed to do something. Maybe it was about contribution to the planet and all of a sudden you wanted to get up and do something. Maybe it's people. Whoever it is, think about the people who really move and motivate you to think and act differently.

Now think about this. When do you do your best work? When do you feel the best? What time of day do you feel the best? I'm talking about where you feel healthy. When do you feel your absolute best? What time of day is that? What type of activities make you feel your best? It might be working out, sometimes it might be. I'm really in the zone. You're spending some quiet time away with God or your creator. Maybe it's that time with your kids. Maybe it's that romantic time when you're spending time with your significant other. Think about those types of activities. Think about the place. Where's the place where you feel most alive? Where's the place you feel most in touch with yourself? You feel good about yourself and want to position yourself in a different way when you go there. For me, it's the water. If I go near a boat or down to the beach, I feel really good. I feel like I can start thinking and hearing things different.

The reason I bring things up is this is another way to set ourselves up to win. Maybe we just have to set some time to do some of these activities, spend some time around these people. If you've got somebody that really inspires you, go to YouTube, type in their name, and watch 4 or 5 videos of them. Maybe have 2 or 3 favorites that you can just go to.

Not too long ago I was watching one of the coolest things;

I was watching this video of Ronald Reagan doing his speech of tear down this wall. I watched Martin Luther King give his I have a Dream speech. I watched John F. Kennedy give his speech. Folks, those move me. Those are some things that are really cool things that happened. If you can tap into those and those move you to a place of action and a different place in your head, it's going to be amazing to see what that does for you. Once you get in that spot, it's so much easier to go the gym and do the things that are necessary. We've got to position ourselves to win and take these steps. Now, what if you were driving along the road and a car came into your lane. What's the typical response? The typical response is your idiot. I want to encourage you to do an untypical response. Do something to the degree that when you do it you recognize it. That was a conscious decision, a conscious effort to be a better person. When you do that even the smallest thing will have a huge effect on you. One thing I give the explanation of is if you walk along and see a piece of trash, pick it up. If you see a piece of paper on the ground, what does it cost you to pick it up? It costs you nothing, but you know what it does? It starts bolstering your psychology, the way you feel about yourself. I notice that time and time again to the point where I now pick it up by habit. I don't do it all the time, but I do try and do it a lot more than I used to do it. The cool thing is every time I've done it I notice I feel a little bit better.

Tell me something, what was something you've done

recently that made you feel better about yourself? Made you feel better about yourself. What was it? Was it picking up a piece of trash? Was it letting someone over in traffic? Was it a random act of kindness? A random act of kindness. It could be something so simple that you just walked next door and carried in the neighbors trash cans. What if you carried in the neighbors trash cans and never told a soul? What if you knew a family or some friends that were going through financial struggles and you just bought them a bag of groceries and left them on the porch with no expectation of them knowing who did it?

Sometimes when we do things like that we get the greatest amount of benefit from it because we start to feel better about ourselves. When you feel better about yourself, isn't it true that you do better work? You perform at a higher level. You also contribute at a higher level. If you feel your best and you're performing at your best, you're also contributing to the world at large at a higher level.

I said this a few months ago and I think it's so true. Every moment that you and I do not perform at our highest level, we don't live out our passion, and create that passion within our lives; the world operates from a deficit. Let's not let the world operate from a deficit because of us. Let's go out and live our lives in such a way that we create this intense desire. We have this commitment, we have this desire, and now we're setting ourselves up to win on a daily basis with consistent and persistent small little actions.

You know, the pilot that landed miracle on Hudson, the airplane that landed on the Hudson, one of the great quotes that came out of that was they asked him how you knew what to do. He said because of all my training and the thousands of hours I'd done, I'd made enough deposits over the course of time that when it came time for a big withdrawal it was there. These are the little deposits we're making in the course of our days. What can you do this morning that will position you and make you feel a little bit better so you perform differently during the rest of the day? The little things that we're doing, we're making those small deposits so we can get the big results.

I'm not saying that any of this is going to make all your problems go away, it doesn't. Anyone that tells you that is lying. What it does it is helps you to handle those problems differently and better and more effectively when they do occur.

I'm the last one to tell you that life is perfect. I'm the last one to tell you that life is easy. I'm the last one to tell you don't worry about it everything's going to be fine. There are things that will go array if we don't change things. How can you position yourself for the most effective day, for the most effective moment? When you walk into a meeting, don't you want it to be the most effective meeting? Of course you do. What does it look like to you? Well, it may look like you're going to have to think about it differently. What can I do to position myself so when I go into that meeting I've got the greatest results, the greatest amount of energy, what is it that you're going to do? Or do you walk into a meeting and go here's another meeting. I kind of figured that we weren't going to get that deal; I figured that my wife was going to yell at me, I figured my kids were going to screw up.

We've got to position ourselves so that when we walk into our meetings, have these discussions with people, when we're going about our lives personal or business, we've got to set ourselves up and build those blocks one step at a time so as we go about our day we're living at a higher level.

Think about the pictures, music, movies, and the people that really inspire you. Maybe you begin your day with that. Maybe during lunch you are really struggling and I'm going to take this time and set myself up to win. I'm going to position myself in a position where I can win. Think about your time of day. When do you feel your best? The types of activities that make you feel your best. Whatever it is for you, think about those things and put yourself in that time of day, around those activities that you enjoy, and the places that will inspire you and help you set up your place to win.

Maybe every morning I just begin with a watching of a song that's played with some background video on the water. Can you see how I'm tying the music in with the video? Maybe it's one of my artists that have done that.

When I do that, I feel different. It's positioning me to win. What actions can you take today? Maybe they're the actions of just letting somebody over in your lane when you don't want to. When you're pulling into a parking lot and somebody's pulling out, rather than get mad at them for not seeing you, you let them go. Maybe picking up a piece of trash, bringing in the trash cans, smiling at somebody.

Whatever it is, I want you to really hone in on the things you can do today to really bring about the best position to win in every area of your life. Whether it's health and vitality, business, whatever it is. Position yourself to win with small actions each and every day. Enjoy your next level.

SESSION FOUR: MONITORING YOUR DIALOGUE

Hey guys, Bob Donnell, Welcome to Day 4 of creating your winning inner game. Day 4 is all about monitoring your inner and external dialogue. If you've made it this far, you've already been through commitment which was day one, day two -desire, and day three was all about setting yourself up to win. Now we're talking about monitoring your dialogue. I've got to tell you, this is tough. It's not as tough to monitor your external dialogue as it is your internal dialogue. Now let me let you in on a secret, your internal dialogue is just as powerful, if not more powerful, as your external dialogue.

We've all been told all the things, don't say anything if you can't say anything nice. We've all had these clichés about guarding your tongue. Even the bible talks about guarding your tongue. What I want to talk to you about is guarding your thoughts, even the words you say to yourself, even the words you say in private.

There was a great sitcom I watched with Matt Labonke. Matt Labonke played Joey. It was a spinoff of friends, and he went on and created this show called Joey. He was an actor and he was trying out for a part. It was really funny because he went to this audition, and while he's sitting out in the hallway he's thinking about all these things that he needs to think about, but he's also thinking about well you're no good, that guy's better looking, that guy's got a bigger resume. He started psyching himself out.

Now if you've ever been in sports, you know what that's like. Maybe you've been in a business negotiation, or just wanted to go out on a date with someone and asking them out and you psyched out. That's what happened to Joey. What happened is he went in and as he began to do the monologue, as he was doing it he started flailing around and he started talking to himself and oh see they don't like you, you have no talent whatsoever.

Guess what, he didn't get the part. Was that a surprise? No, it wasn't. Probably wasn't even a surprise to Joey because he had already told himself he wasn't getting the part. How many things are going on in your life right now that are strictly because of the internal dialogue that you've got going on? That inner game that we're talking about, that internal dialogue is kicking your butt.

How many times do you think about I'm just not smart enough, that's not the way I was raised, that guy's so much better at that, or that guys prettier? How many times do you have those thoughts? I guarantee it's thousands a day if you're not guarding your internal dialogue.

Let's think about this. There are some great things that we can do to exercise and really create an internal dialogue. Have you ever heard the nursery rhyme Sally by the seashore picking up seashells? You cannot say that without almost cracking a smile or laughing. Why is that? It's something about that dialogue. What I want to explain to you is that that same internal dialogue that has negative consequences can have a positive consequence. You have to change that internal dialogue on a consistent and persistent basis. A lot of times we say things that are self-deprecating. This doesn't look that good, it wasn't me, I'm not that talented, it was everyone else.

I'm not talking about being humble. I'm not talking about having a healthy understanding of who you are in the midst of the bigger schemes of things. Do you have the ability to monitor that dialogue and make it healthy? Healthy is not self-deprecating. Healthy is accepting. Healthy is realizing our potential. Realizing the steps that you need to take. It's that inner game, creating an inner dialogue.

I can guarantee you this, if you want to try this as an exercise here's a great exercise. Sit here and think negative thoughts for five minutes. Five minutes will literally shift your state. Stop at the end of those five minutes, and I want you to write down about how you feel about yourself, your spouse, your finances, your business, think about that. Now, I want you to take the next 5 minutes and think positive thoughts, things that really stir you to the core, exciting emotionally charged things that make you happy. Think about your kids, when they were little, the times that you played with them, and the times that you laughed. Whatever it is, think about those amazing things, those words that that represented. Think about those words. Love, laughter, happiness, joy, peace. 5 minutes, same amount of time. How do you feel about your spouse, how do you feel about yourself? How do you feel about your business, your current situations? I guarantee there will be a vast difference, and it all was created by thought. That internal dialogue that you were having.

Do you realize that people physiologically have responses to the way that they're speaking? So when you're speaking in a nice, calm, passive, tone. What happens? Your breathing changes. Your speech patterns change. You become better at annunciating. There are a lot of things that change when you change your dialogue.

Now, your physiology is being affected. We're going to talk about physiology in the next couple of days, but right now I want you to really focus on this internal dialogue as well as your external dialogue.

Do you ever find yourself saying, "No, I can't," or "I'm not that smart"? That internal dialogue is kicking your butt every single day. I can guarantee it because it's kicked mine; it's kicked everyone I know, including the President of the United States. What I'm talking about right now is going to be so revolutionary if you can grasp this, monitoring your internal dialogue.

What does that look like? When you're about to say something, you're having this thought about saying it, and you've got to turn to it and say I'm not going to say that, or give it any more thought. I'm going to change the way I'm thinking and what I'm saying. Is that something that you can do? Absolutely. Is it something you will do? I don't know. That's something that you've got to decide right now.

Again, it's going to boil down to the commitment that you make to make this happen. Are you willing to be committed to that, or are you willing to let it continue? It's going to boil down to the results that you want. Are you committed? Are you?

Listen to this. Henry Ford said this great statement. Whether you think you can or think you can't, you're right. You've got to realize that this internal dialogue is killing you. If you do not monitor it, it will literally destroy your business, your health, your finance, your family.

We haven't even talked about external. When you say

something with conviction and passion, your emotion is there. Everything changes with your physiology, the way your eyes and pupils dilate. When you put your shoulders forward and talk in a monotone voice, you begin to have that same effect. Monitoring your dialogue, monitoring your tone, is so vital. It's going to be absolutely revolutionary for you creating a winning game.

Now look, you've spent the time, you've spent 3 days; this is day 4 that you're focusing on creating a winning inner game. Don't forget, this is going to take some work, some time, some energy to make this shift. Every time you begin to think or say something that is negative, that's not serving you. If it's not serving you, write it down. What am I saying? Think about why I am saying it. Write down what you were about to think or say and then say why did I say that? Then ask yourself, what does that do for me?

Folks, I'm telling you that if you do this, if you spend this amount of time, do this inner work on your dialogue, start monitoring it. Find someone that is an accountability partner. You've got to get it to the point where you start doing it.

Are there some triggers? Are there some things that are happening that right before you say it you feel it? What you want to do is you want to start identifying what those things are. As you get better at identifying what those things are, then you will be able to shift, literally in a moment's notice change that dialogue. I feel this, I know what the outcome's going to be, and it's not going to be good. It's not going to be the outcome that's serving me.

Think about that. Think about the triggers, the emotions, the feelings. We've talked about music; we've talked about watching movies, associating our mental and emotional state with all of these external factors. What are those triggers? What will make me feel positive or negative? Start saying, why am I about to say this, or why am I thinking this? How is it serving me? How is it helping me? What are those triggers so you can catch them on your own?

Guys, I know that if you can do this work, if you spend the time on it, I can guarantee you that as you begin to shift; you'll begin to say things that are more serving to you, and get better results. Go ahead, do the exercise. Make sure that you're staying committed to yourself. This is all about you creating the winning inner game that's going to give you the results you want, and the results that everyone else around you needs. Go ahead, get started, and enjoy your next level.

SESSION FIVE: SEE THINGS AS THEY TRULY ARE

Well guys, you made it. Day 5, congratulations. There are a lot of people that didn't. There are a lot of people that bought this program and said this is just too tough. I don't want have to be that committed. I want to really let you know that I appreciate the fact that you made it to day five. We've only got two days left, but day 5 is pivotal because after yesterday when we talked about monitoring our dialogue, did you do it? Did you find yourself thinking about other things? Were you listening to the words other people were saying? Did you start to realize that internal dialogue that's going on? Did you realize the external dialogue? I bet you did, and I guarantee that if you continue that, it will serve you well in every aspect of your life.

Now let me ask you this, today were you monitoring your

language? Here's the pivotal point that's going to be so valuable for you, and that's to be able to understand things as they truly are. Not better than they are, and not worse than they are. Let me explain. There are a lot of statements that people make. Things like I have to start over again, I lost everything I own. In that relationship I took nothing. It's not true is it? When you walk out of a relationship with someone, or a business, or opportunities, you take with you experience, knowledge, a greater understanding of you and other people. All these different things, newfound knowledge, relationships.

I had a coaching client tell me, "Bob, I'm starting my business all over; I have to start from scratch." No you're not; you've got vendors that you've already got in place. You've got experience that you've been running this business. You've already got a lot of contacts. You've got a greater understanding of the market than anyone who is just coming into the market, trying to start your business. They would be starting from nothing and you have a huge leg up on them.

Don't make it worse than it is, but also don't make it better than it is. A lot of times people say, "Bob, if I lose my job, I'll find another one." No, don't do that to yourself. Your psychology is supporting the fact of losing a job. What you need to do is create an attitude that I need to do everything I can to make sure that doesn't happen. Things happen beyond our control, but as soon as you say well if I lose it, you're allowing it to happen within your control. I'm not talking about when someone comes up and just fires you, I'm talking about things that you do have control over. Don't allow your psychology to support them more than its supporting you. Psychology has to be strong enough to support the efforts. If it's not supporting you it's extorting you. Don't make it softer than it is.

People say I'm driving this car because it's a good car. Just in the way they're saying it you can see there's something wrong. I'm not saying the car is the issue; their psychology about the car is the issue. If they had $50,000 in the bank would they be driving that car? Maybe not. So again, making it too easy, too soft, to where they don't feel the pain. Maybe they should say this car's great and I'm grateful for this car, but I have a better car in mind and I want to do that. Or maybe they're saying I'm doing okay, I'm not obese, but I want to be in great health. I'm going to take extra measures to lose weight. We've got to get to the point where we don't just soften it to where it gives us permission to not take action. Don't make it better than it is, but don't make it worse than it is.

Now let me ask you, today, give me the situation that you're most struggling with. When you go to bed, it keeps you up at night. When you wake up, it makes you tired. What is that thing that's kicking your butt day in and day out? On a scale of 1 to 10, how bad is it? Be truthful with yourself. On a scale of 1 to 10, it's a 9. What evidence do I have to support that it's a 9? Or maybe you're saying it's not that big of a deal, I can get another job tomorrow. So it's not a big deal, it might be a level 2. What's the evidence that supports that? If you had to get a job tomorrow, how long would it take to get a job? How long would it take you to get back on your feet? Don't soften it to the point where you don't take action, but don't make it worse than it is.

Folks, there are so many opportunities for us, but if we fail to recognize and create a sense of urgency for ourselves, then a lot of times we miss those opportunities. Think about how you can create a sense of urgency about something that maybe you're not making very important right now. The reason you're not making it important isn't because it's not important. You want to give yourself permission to not work; you want to give yourself permission to not have to deal with the struggle, the hard situation. You're just giving yourself permission by making it not important.

The opposite is you make things to important. You start majoring on minor issues, and all of a sudden the minor issues become huge. Why? They weren't to begin with, but we created this about them. Sometimes we do that in relationships. I bet you do this when you're thinking about buying something.

Have you ever thought well I really don't need to spend the money on that, but then you start rationalizing? If I bought this software it would save me time and I could be more productive and make more money. You buy the software and bring it home and nothing changes. What happened is you went into a mode where you tried to justify and make something that was a minor issue a major issue. You start building to the point where you convinced yourself to buy the software. Whatever it is, think about it. How many times do you build it up the point so you can justify?

Don't make things better than they are, but don't make things worse than they are. Be honest with who you are in that given situation. Be honest about what you want. Ask these questions: Is it really that bad? Is it really okay if I get fired?

Think about those things then ask this question: What can I do to make this better? What can I do to make it stronger and healthier and really produce the outcome that I want? What is it that you want? Think about the situation that you're in. If I can make this ideal, what would it look like? Hmm, am I doing what I need to do to make the picture perfect happen, or am I just willing to settle for a picture that is blurry or has lost its color or has been torn, or a picture that has faded. We've got to get back to the point where we create a sense of urgency. We're not talking about majoring on the minor; we're talking about making things that are important. Health, psychical fitness, doesn't wait until crisis. Take a good look at exactly what's going on.

I know that if you do this, think about your situation, whatever it is, someone's died, bankruptcy, car repossession, don't make it better than it is, don't make it worse than it is. Be honest with yourself and in your family. Sometimes we'll say something and catch each other and try and justify. Hopefully we call each other to maybe it shouldn't be okay. Maybe it shouldn't be okay that I only have x amount of money set aside for my children's education. Maybe it shouldn't be okay that I don't make as many sales calls as I should. Then we need to create that sense of urgency behind it. Is my behavior supporting the outcome that I want? If it's not, focus on how things truly are. Not better than they are, not worse than they are, do the exercises, think about them clearly, and I can guarantee that you're going to have a healthier perspective of what the situation is, and be able to deal with it more effectively. Don't forget, do the exercises, tomorrow, day 6. Enjoy your next level.

SESSION SIX: CHANGE YOUR PHYSIOLOGY

Well, you made it to day six. Day six. I don't know about you, but the first 5, if you have been doing the exercises, you have gotten some create information and gotten some great skill sets that will serve you well in every aspect of business and in life for the rest of your life. The coolest thing about that is that it's something that you're learning and taking control of that's going to serve you and your community for years to come. The skills you're learning are things that you can incorporate into your daily life that will truly benefit you and are in your immediate circle and the world at large. The better you become, the more effective you become at running your company, transcends out to everyone in the world.

Welcome to Day 6. Did you do the exercises in Day 5? If you didn't, go back and do them. I know that you'll get maximum benefit from that. If you stop and think about the benefits of what was going on in Day 5. Think about if you didn't do the exercises, what's that about? Do you think that it's lazy, that you didn't want to? Do you think that it was too difficult? There's something in your internal dialogue, your inner game is defeating you. It's extorting the unlimited possibilities that you have for business. The best way to take control and get your inner game to start supporting you is do the exercises. I guarantee you when you go and crush out that tendency to not do the things that were difficult, you're going to build up your psychology. If you have done them, congratulations, we're on to Day 6.

Day 6 is all about physiology. Physiology literally determines everything that we do. 99% of the time it will determine how effective we are at something. It doesn't necessarily change how we read, but it certainly can. Think about this, physiology has everything to do with how you breathe, your patterns, your nervous energy, everything is included. Physiology is biochemistry. Your physiology is one of the most determining and strongest indicators of the effect on your mood and emotional resources, as well as personal motivation. A person's state of mind is heavily influence by the physiology, by what's going on.

Let me ask you this, right now are you sitting forward? Is your speech pattern slow? Are you tired? If you're tired, you've probably already dropped your head. If you're sitting in a desk your elbow are on the desk. The reason is your physiology is supporting how you're feeling. If you're not feeling happy, if you're feeling depressed, it's very common for your shoulders to slump forward. Your breathing becomes shallower. Your tone goes down. You speak slower. That's all physiology. If you want to change your state, change your physiology. Your physiology can be as simple as sitting up straight, putting both feet on the ground, shoulders up, breathe. Maybe hit your fist. Do something that once you start movement, you'll start to feel different. Because you're changing your state of mind, your state of mind changes.

There are so many reasons why, but I can give you more documentation if you want it. By in large what you need to understand is your physiology is either kicking you in the butt, or supporting you to great new levels. Day 6 is all about making committed decision to yourself to get the results that you want by taking charge once and for all to say when I start to feel depressed, I'm going to do something about it. You may not be able to change your external circumstances, but you can change your internal dialogue. One of the best ways I know is to change your physiology.

Most people are living a life of apathy right now, and because of that apathy we're getting into all kinds of situations. Apathy will destroy people's lives. Right now I'm challenging you; I want to encourage you, to start with your physiology. You've got to start with the way you talk, but you've also got to start with the way you stand.

Have you ever noticed someone who stands upright, and you go man they've got great posture? They probably have great posture for a different reason than you think. Sometimes they have literally shaped themselves, decided that they needed to make a conscious effort of how they stand so they started to get different results I had a meeting with Brandon Tarkoff who used to be the head of NBC Studios. By chance meeting, I was actually standing next to those gentleman at an event and I just looked at him and man he's go at great suit, he was so professional, so put together. When they said our speaker today is Brandon Tarkoff, Brandon was standing next to me and walked up. I didn't know who he was at the time, but I sat there and thought wow, what kind of presence did he exude in that room?

Now, I can tell you, it made a lasting impression on me. This was in 1989, and this is 2010. Another gentleman who just has great physiology is this guy names Will Smith. Will Smith is a phenomenal guy, and I've been around him three or four times. Every time he's got this warmth, this smile, his swagger, this ability to connect with people. The high reason because he's got a great ability to connect with people is his physiology.

I was at the Grammy's in the green room and there was a bunch of rappers in there. Everyone was silent, no one was talking. When Will Smith walked in, everyone's eyes wandered. He introduced himself. I am here. I'm not here to become a fixture of the room; I'm here to change the dynamics of the room.

What are your goals when you walk into a room? What are you goals when you sit down at your desk? What are your goals when you walk out to speak with your family? What are your goals when you go to a business meeting? Do you have specific goals, and does your physiology represent that? What would you say if somebody said I don't know man, I'm just so excited? Things are great.

Have you ever heard the statement, hey could you tell your face? That's the bottom line. A lot of times our physiology isn't supporting what we're trying to accomplish. You've got to make sure you are protected. Everyone's heard the statement laughter is the best medicine. Laughter does have some great benefits that really help you. If laughter can do that and it's been considered good medicine, think about it. The opposite can be true. Poor sleep, poor diet, poor posture. All that boils down to disease. We've got to start thinking about it from the standpoint of when you start to feel down, overwhelmed, depressed, you've got to change your physiology. Your physiology will be the most important thing in determining and changing your attitude right off the bat. That quick it can happen.

Here are your exercises. I want you to spend the next 10 minutes writing down 3 or 4 things you can do to immediately change the way you feel. Maybe it's do some pushups, visualization, whatever it is that makes you start thinking about your physiology that makes you cognizant about your breathing, about the tonality of your voice, your commitment level. Everything is going to be showing up in your physiology. If it's not, you need to change your physiology so it begins to support you. Day 7 is coming up. Stay tuned. The reason physiology is so important today is because tomorrow I want you mentally there spiritually there, emotionally there, and physiologically there. I want you to sit up straight and come to tomorrow's session with intensity. Finish this session off really strong so you can get the results you want. Get started on those exercises and implement them today to help you increase and get the long-standing possibilities and ideas you've always wanted. Enjoy your next level.

SESSION SEVEN: THE POWER OF ASSOCIATION

Welcome to day 7, Day 7 of winning your inner game. I've got to congratulate you, because there are a lot of people that will never make it to day 7. I want to congratulate you for taking that time, putting forward that energy, and putting forward that extra effort in order to be the person that you were designed to be. The person that you know inside in your core that you really are, but haven't been living to that capacity.

I want to congratulate you. Welcome to day 7. Day 7 is all about association. It's been said that if you take the 5 people who you spend the most amount of time, energy, and resources with, you'll probably fall in the middle of them regarding your income and your lifestyle. For some people, they say I need some new friends then. But really what I want you to do is start thinking from the standpoint of who are you spending them most time and resources with. Yes your kids, spouse, and parents obviously effect how you believe.

When you have time to spend with somebody, somebody to hang out with, who are those people that you spend the time with? Do those people have the lifestyle that you want? If you were to fall in the middle of it, if you were to take those people, would you be happy with the income and lifestyle? If you could wake up tomorrow and do anything, what would you want to do? If you could be anyone in your life, who would you want to be? I'm not talking about being someone other than you, but their lifestyle, their income levels, the relationships they have, the businesses they have? Who are those people that you really respect?

Let me ask you this, are you spending time with the 5 people that are really influencing, are those people living the kind of lives that you want. I know this is tough. I'm not trying to make light of it. What I'm saying is we've got to be concerned about who we spend our time with. We're so concerned about who our kids spend time with. We even tell them that you can be guilty by association. Doesn't the same principal apply to us? Of course it does. So we've got to be very concerned but we've also got to be conscious about which we spend our time with.

Now let me ask you this, if you want results, and you want the kind of results that you've always wanted rather than the results that you're getting, it's going to take a shift not only in the way you think, it's going to take a shift in the beliefs that you have, the actions that you take so you can get the different results. We've got to look at all 7 modules to understand and help you create a winning inner game.

Study after study indicates that our immediate peers are very influential in creating and/or supporting our incomes, our lifestyles, our business, our language, our belief systems, as well as our patterns. As parents we tell our children this, why don't we apply it for ourselves?

Why this is difficult is because it's comfortable to be around someone that doesn't shake or rattle our belief, that doesn't hold us accountable to a higher level. How often would you want to look in the mirror to gauge how you look if you were looking at a mirror that was crashed? Unfortunately that's what we do a lot with our friends. They don't help us understand who we really are and what we're really about. What they give us is a distorted view, and because of that, we never get clarity on where we could rise up, where we could live at a higher level, and where we can't. We become like those people because anything opposite would be opposition, intrusive, abrasive. We resist that so we start to become like our peers.

I want you to think today, who are the five people, not including your kids and spouse, which you spend the most amount of time with? I want you to look at their incomes, their lifestyles, their relationships, their spiritual convictions, the way they contribute to people, and even their health and fitness and say if I were to fall in the middle of those 5 people, would I be happy with that? If you wouldn't be happy and if you're not happy with that, I want you to start raising yourself to a higher level.

Ask yourself this: who are the people that you respect most in any given area? Say, health and fitness? Who would those people choose to spend their lunch hour with, their evenings with? Same thing with relationships. Who would they spend time with? They would probably choose to spend time with different people that you are spending time with. If it fits, you've got to wear it. I want something bigger and better. Be very clear on the 5 people that you're spending the most amount of time and energy with. Are they getting the kind of results that you want or are they getting similar results? It's time to step up, raise the bar, leading and thinking differently, associating with people that will push you to believe differently.

Look I don't know if you have a mentor or a coach, I know I've been your coach for the past 7 days. If you don't have a coach, I recommend that you get one. Every successful person in professional athletes to business has a coach. Someone that looks them in the eye and says you're better than that, you can do better than that, and you can be better than that. I would love to be that person for you. If you go to the website and subscribe, we can point you to somebody that can help you with that. Because of the next level program, we have a membership program. Every week we hold an online meeting where I spend about 30-40 minutes talking to you about your inner game and your life and shedding light on aspect that help you raise it to the next level. It's inexpensive, $97 to start and $29.99 a month. It's inexpensive but it will provide lasting value for you, your family, your businesses, your colleagues, everyone in your live. Go to thenextlevel4results.com. Join the membership. If you need a mentor, go to the coaching program and sign up. We've got a live event coming up near you. Check out the nearest events we've got. Again, this is Bob Donnell of Next Level 4 Success and Next Level 4 results, and I want to thank you for the privilege and the honor to be your coach for the last 7 days. Remember, this is not the end, it's just the beginning. Step up, raise the bar, become the person you were designed to be. Again, Bob Donnell, nextlevel4results.com, enjoy your next level.

ABOUT THE AUTHOR

In the growing world of personal development and strategic coaching, few people are as well respected and adored as Bob Donnell. Combining a heart centered authenticity with winning strategies for, business and life, Bob has separated himself as a true leader in the industry.

Having cultivated an entrepreneurial spirit at an early age, he started his first non-profit organization at 18 focused on helping at-risk families in crisis. From there, Bob made an impact in the world of sales and a management until he decided to devote the entirety of his life to helping others in transformation. That road, however, wasn't arrived at easily.

From growing up in poverty to never knowing his father; from the untimely loss of his mother during his teen years to tragically losing his 3 year-old daughter in a freakish car accident, Bob decided that life is too short to continue struggling. He has since devoted his life and business to helping others design their life by getting the results they've been wanting to see.

Now, as a leading Results Strategist, Bob continues to work with entrepreneurs, sales professionals, celebrities, professional athletes as well as any who desires to take their life and business to the next level.

Bob's body of work includes authoring several books, recording audio programs, hosting radio programs and. He also hosts a weekly live video streaming, interactive program with members
worldwide. Bob has worked with a distinguished list of clients including Coldwell Banker, Long Beach Grand Prix, Arbonne International, ReMax, World Ventures, Oakley Inc., Pre-Paid Legal,. In addition, Bob has loved working within the entertainment industry; the Academy Awards, the WB Music Awards, Victor Awards, The Grammy's and, as a result, has been able to interact with and study some of the great artists in the world including Garth Brooks, The Backstreet Boys, Reba McIntyre, and Will Smith.

The culmination of Bob's 20-year career has led him to create Next Level 4 Success which continues to stand as a beacon for those desperately looking to take their lives to the next level. His expertise in knowing the human condition and the keys to getting stronger, faster results sets him apart from his peers.

Simply put, Bob Donnell gets results. If you're looking to take your life or business to the next level, there's no better time than the present to start getting results that speak for themselves.

Are you ready?

NOTES

Made in the USA
San Bernardino, CA
19 July 2013